wild love raging

wild love raging

JOANNE DZIERZA

First Printing, 2019

ISBN: 978-1-9990517-0-9

for those who have tasted magic

you

no one tells you
the truth about soulmates
that when they tear the veil
of mundanity to show you
how beautiful life can be
you end up spending
the rest of your days
in search of the same clarity
coming up short
unable to return to any
semblance of normalcy
of life before them

-the truth about soulmates

i see you making eyes at me
don't think that i don't know
she wears a pretty diamond ring
but it's with her back at home
we edge a little closer
dancing on a line
i think we're onto something
pretending you are mine

-taken

you smile at me from across the room
while she dances there in front of you
i hate that i love these stolen looks
when we do the things we shouldn't do

-you don't love her

desire tugs us
like we're nothing more
than marionettes
my attempts are feeble
rejecting the pull
and i'm helplessly led
right back to you

-it's not my fault

when our eyes meet
i feel canyons grow
soaring before me
vastly beautiful
and without notice
by no push or pull
i'm soaring with them
in endless fall

-canyons

prudence, how quickly you vanish
as soon as darkness veils the light
my mind finds ways to succumb
to the whim of this wild aching
forbidden has made a beast of me

-wild love raging

i will not apologize
for the truths
i cause you to face

-divisive

you're dressed in
that blue shirt again
the one i really love
does she know
you wore it
for me tonight
and that later
i'll take it off

-the secrets you keep

nobody knows
the things we know
the truth is nestled
somewhere underneath
the layers of these sheets

-our sacred place

i love how effortlessly
you find the valleys of my hips
the way you hold them so carefully
suspended at your fingertips
my skin barely feels you
as your hands gently run
across my fragile places
while our lines blur into one

-gentle yearning

let me help you
see yourself
through my eyes
you'll be amazed
at the details
you find

-a different perspective

sometimes
the sun paints the sky
so beautifully
that you don't want it to leave
this is precisely
what your light does to me

-sunsets remind me of you

see what your light
has done to me?
look how it leaves me exposed
and now my darkness
has no where to go

-*exposed*

we have a love that
takes no convincing
like how the waves
get weak for the shore
they always find strength
to come back for more

-waves

we love and we love
pouring out every ounce we have
until these hearts are bone dry
until it hurts to give
as quickly as these lungs
reach for air
so they exhale
spilling onto you
we love and we love
because it is true

-oxygen

does your lover write for you?
is she compelled
to draw ink from her veins
to paint you on paper
stopping only to revel
in the beauty
of the markings on the page?
you deserve nothing less
so until then
i'll continue
to fill in the blanks

-attention

a word of caution
against falling for poets
true, you will be loved passionately
with undivided attention
but don't be surprised
when down the road
fragments of your soul
are strewn across their pages

-inspiration

we seek meaning
in constellations
like the stars know
something
more than us
this is how
i search your eyes
desperate
to connect the dots

-constellations

it is a priceless gift to be seen
sweeter still, through your eyes
i love how effortlessly
i am known by you

-layers

the space there was blissful
for the fleeting moment
that we forgot about time
and its power
to take things away

-bliss

on the nights i can't fall asleep
i picture me on your chest
counting rests between the beats
sinking into those spaces
like it's the only place
i'm meant to be

-favourite place

i could find a piece of you
in the smallest speck of stardust
making its way determined
amidst the vast abyss above
i could find a piece of you
in the crescent of a wave
leaping with life into its lover
and just so departing into the deep
i find you in every fibre of this fickle life
in the wildest and most fragile places
bursting into existence at every breath
and collapsing together on the exhale

-i find you

i catch myself
in awe of the tracks
you leave all over me
i fear it'll take time
to erase marks like
these

-*imprints*

thank you
for the countless nights
you helped
me survive
for being one
of the reasons
i'm still alive

-you saved me

you may never know
how gently i am wrapped
like a bow around your fingers
terrified of the next time
i might come undone

-the unraveling

just say the words
i'll bend
i'll bruise
oh eager love
why do you hurt

-bruises

am i enough
should i shovel up my depths
to bring to shallow surface
all the intricate and cleverly laced
parts of me to prove it
i can only hope
that if you start at the edges
and carefully travel inward
you'll find yourself amazed
at the complexity of
the signature i've created
i'll lay myself out
so that your eyes might catch
my virtues
like monuments contrasted
against a steady horizon
don't wait to marvel
for this is temporary
and once my insides decide
that they are too tired
only my stone will publish me then
and i hope eloquently

-this is temporary

death brings me no fear
because you'll be
the last thought on my mind
and i can't think
of a sweeter way to go

-final thoughts

you believe in an afterlife
up among the stars
but your eternity
is here on earth
i made it for you
with these
words

-you will live forever

i threw my fists at your chest
but they were halted by your softness
my scathing voice accused you
while you held me in the darkness
i'll never forget this moment
when my rage was met with kindness
you said you'd always love me
this was you keeping your promise

-unconditional

you never flinch
at the sight of my chaos
instead you brave it gracefully
like maybe you've tasted it before
like it reminds you of your own

-that makes two

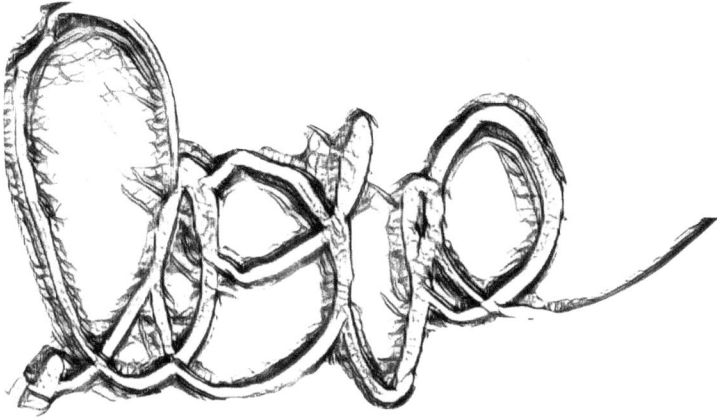

maybe
the world wasn't built
for people like us
maybe
we need to change it
with our love

-love always wins

i wish that my heart
worked like traffic lights
stopping accidents

-red means stop

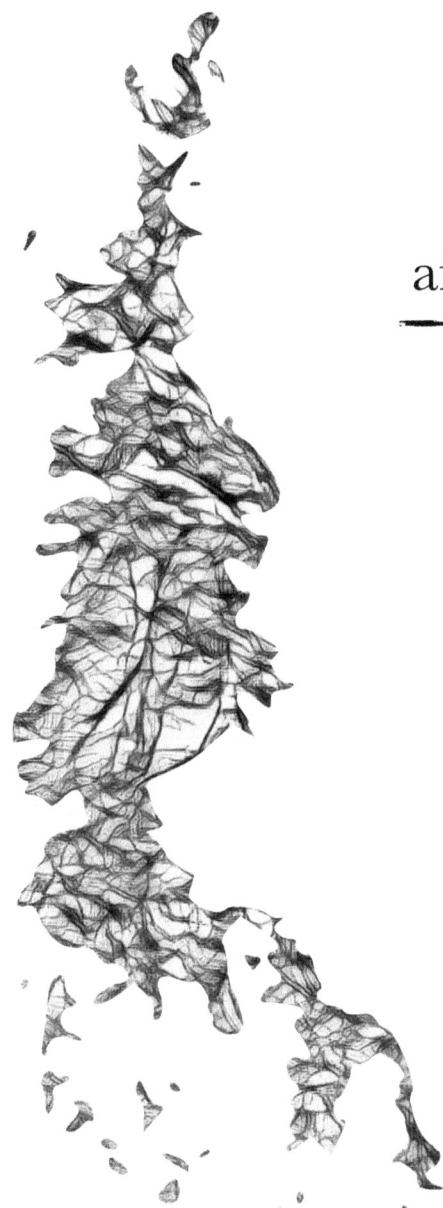

after you

they say that
she loves you
and that
you love her too
my mind ingests this truth
the way flesh devours a bullet
seemingly slow, yet
changed forever

-bullets

you cannot lose
what was never yours
how could i forget
you were always hers

-wedding rings

you hold on
while telling me to let go
i have scars on my wrists
from this tug of war
love me or leave me
these in-betweens
are hurting

-decide

you can say you don't love me
you can swear it for her sake
you can repeat, repeat, repeat,
it's okay!
this secret is ours to keep
i'll never tell a soul
what your eyes say to me

-i know the truth

everyone
has something to say
about our love
how can they possibly
think they know me
better than i know myself?
more so
how did i let them
speak to me
as if they do?

-strangers

here i am at the end
here i am alone
afraid
looking for anything
to fill the vacancy
how do you tell someone
that you need them
when they've
already
walked away?

-*come back*

there's freedom in impulse
until you're shackled
with consequence

-discernment

i used to think
that being next to him
was the safest place on earth
until i learned
that sometimes
it's the closest ones
that turn their backs on you

-trust issues

the stars must have been curious
of the light between us
the last night you held me
we could've made the universe blind
laughing till our stomachs ached
reflections of heaven in our eyes
but as every eve braces for sun
and the night sky slips away
so the end of us has begun
i wait for a new day

-patient

goodbyes remind me
that sustained bliss is an illusion
sorrow always follows

-the exit

i wish i'd run the other way
and ignored his deceiving call
he said my name so beautifully
right before he watched me fall

-delusions

splinters in my skin
from where your hands once slid
i wait for time to slowly pry
every last bit of you out of me

-reminders

i needed you
when the wounds you left
were too deep to clean
trying to find solace
on my bedroom floor
eyes an endless stream
i needed you like oxygen
when my starving veins
were unable to breathe
so don't you dare
ever convince yourself
that you care for me
love doesn't watch the fall
with a thousand scattered pieces
and then choose to leave

-where were you

you said i could keep your heart
but all you left was your sweater
it has since kept me warm
but i think i wore you better

-i want you instead

i let your sweater hold me
because i know you never will again
and i fall apart on Fridays
thinking of how this came to end
wondering how many hours
it will take to feel alright
and how many tears
i'll let myself lose tonight

-it's over

should i be afraid that lately
i can't feel anything at all
or should i celebrate
these fortified walls
no one tells you
how to survive
it's just expected
and running is the
only way that
i know how

-numb

i can't decide
if i should have pride for the way
i've concealed my deepest truths
or be ruined by the ability i have
to deceive my heart
from authenticity
i've gotten so good
at believing the lies
i tell myself

-liar liar

staring at an empty space
the absence in my heart
you said you'd never leave
i wonder where you are
you bathed me in your love
then left me here to drown
and for another blurry night
i suffocate alone
say you won't forget my face
please don't forget my name
tell me you regret everything
about the day you walked away

-please

i beg the stars
for you to return
but they're too busy
to hear my concerns
so i ponder the distance
from me to the moon
and wonder if perhaps
you're pondering too

-let's meet in the sky

i'm terrified that i might spend
the rest of my life
looking for you in their faces
whispering your name in secret
settling for love that is less
than what we had

-why can't i forget you

i'd rather spend my whole life
screaming your name tirelessly
than pretend to be okay
okay is not enough
i want great

-nothing else compares

your roots have devastated my heart's soil
if only i could pinpoint the source
if only i could dig you out
even then, would i be happy?
losing you would mean
losing the best part of me

-roots

i revel in the fleeting bliss
the split second before
i fully shake from slumber
the moment right before
i remember you are gone

-dream state

hands meeting under tables
hearts beating under covers
you touched my bruises so gently
i didn't notice you leaving more
silly girl…
thinking that a man
would honour
everything that lies
beneath this skin

-when will you learn they are savages

i thought by now
i'd have forgotten
the way you played with my hair
like you knew every strand
the way my name sounded sweeter
when it was leaving your lips
the way my heart slightly tightened
when you left me forever
i didn't think i'd keep remembering

-the dark side of memories

the waves never ask the shore
if it's okay to leave
they just come
and go as they please
i see now
that this convenience
is why you wanted me

-the shore is always there

you said one day
you might come back
why do you keep me
hanging
on
like
that?

-tease

just as i ride the high of knowing
that i'm better off without you
i get sideswiped by the pain
of being left behind
and this is exactly
the inconsistency
of self worth
that got me here
in the first place

-weak

you hit me
like lightning
and i'll never
be the same
these scars
remind me
not to dance
in the rain
i'd never
survive
if you
struck again

-lightning

how did i let myself
get so sick of existence?
is it the cruelties endured?
am i being selfish?
maybe
my heart knows
nothing else will ever
satisfy like you do

-the search for meaning

there's nothing like
feeling lonely
when you're not alone

-isolation

i picture a different ending
like the ones in the movies
you'd burst through my door
and kiss me wildly
while between breaths i'd ask
what took you so long

-hollywood love

i keep pouring concrete
over the garden you left behind
but traces of you
always grow through

-pruning

i've been having
some trouble
putting myself
back together
ever since you
undid me at the seams
i think i'll be cleaning
this mess up forever
i can't stop my insides
from dripping

-stitches

i wonder why we romanticize
the tears we shed for lovers
as if we are proud to say
look at all of me
that i am losing for you
it isn't sweet at all
the pieces we'll never retrieve
they do not reflect adoration
but a simple leaking tragedy

-hopeless romantics

there are days
that i remember us fondly
but there is folly in hindsight
forgetting the marks
you left behind
are scars
that reopen
every time my heart starts
beating for something
or someone new

-rose coloured glasses

i still think about
the way you kissed me goodbye
i didn't know then
that it would be the last time
it's tragic to realize
there are limits to love
you would have come back
but i wasn't enough

-the last time

i held your hand picturing the
universe and its brightest stars
smiling at the orchestration
i couldn't believe that history
and its thousands of yearning years
would write us into its narration
and i'm forced to wonder
if loving you was some sort of destiny
or if we were gravely mistaken

-was it a mistake

JOANNE DZIERZA

now that you're gone
i no longer feel
the deep twisted knot
that kept me wondering
if i'd ever hear from you again
and i haven't yet figured out
if that is sweet relief
or a devastating truth

-you left too soon

words can't bear to hold
the weight of our love
so i search for ways
to become what it was
still it will always exist
boldly beyond these efforts

-larger than life

there is no rest for romantics
spilling out eternities
into the pores of lovers
who leave
because even this
was not enough

-exhausted

what freedom can i find
wearing this skin like shackles
no cry for help
can undress me from this
some days i wish
i could carve myself out
and break through these walls
just to prove that
i am so much more
than my flesh and bones

-this body is temporary

i'm still trying
to un-see your soul
but how can i
when it is a reflection
of everything inside of me

-*mirrors*

some relief
accompanying
my last breath
will be in never again
waking to reach
at an empty space
where i so badly
wanted you to be

-the other side

my heart is a host of memories
and i preserve them like artifacts, desperately
these recollections are all i have

-museum

come sorrow
tell me how ruined i will be
i'll retaliate slow
grace will be my
remedy

-grace

the sun is so patient
when clouds linger in the way
she still radiates
on the greyest of days

-keep shining

we waste our energies
demystifying the unknowns
what if everything
we've ever needed
is buried in our depths
yearning to come alive

-don't underestimate yourself

JOANNE DZIERZA

having nothing to lose
resembles boundless freedom
don't be fooled
it is restricted by
a total lack of meaning

-live for something

maybe my legacy isn't
how much i loved you
but the empty space that
leaving me
has left you with

-the things that remain

my mind paints
fictitious pictures
of the people i know
dreamlike and
exaggerated
but reality rarely
reflects them so
this i think
is my biggest flaw

-painful virtues

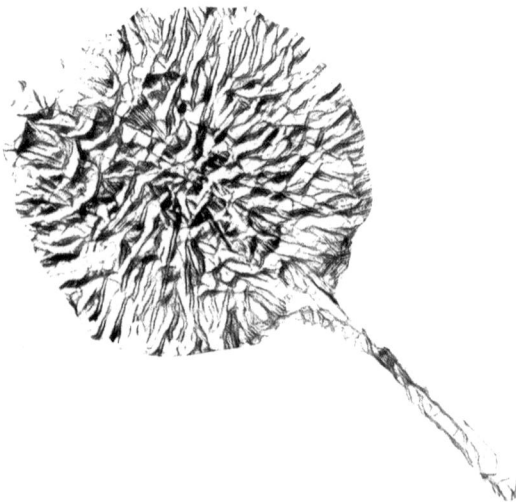

one thing you can count on
is the rain's ability
to melt away masks
and dampen our veils
until it is clear
we are all
collectively
one big
sopping mess

-unified

to be real means
sometimes making concessions
for those caught up in fiction
not every authentic part of you
needs an accurate translation
revel in this power of ambiguity

-don't explain yourself

that's the problem
with pretending to be strangers
facades dissipate when eyes meet
and a deep knowing is spilled out
staining everything anew

-friends to lovers to leavers

i wonder if you feel it too
the sudden halt of time
a million memories relived
in the meeting of our eyes
i've yet to find another man
that shakes me like you do
i hope you understand
i cannot stay
lest i fall madly
back in love with you

-encounters

i spend so much time
fortifying my defences
just to ache as they slip away
instantly taken by the tide
like a castle in the waves
every time i see your face

-i break for you

driving down the same old roads
trying to get somewhere new
chasing after taillights
while the radio sings about you
maybe if i go far enough
i can leave this love behind
maybe there's someone out there
who can get you off my mind

-i need to get away

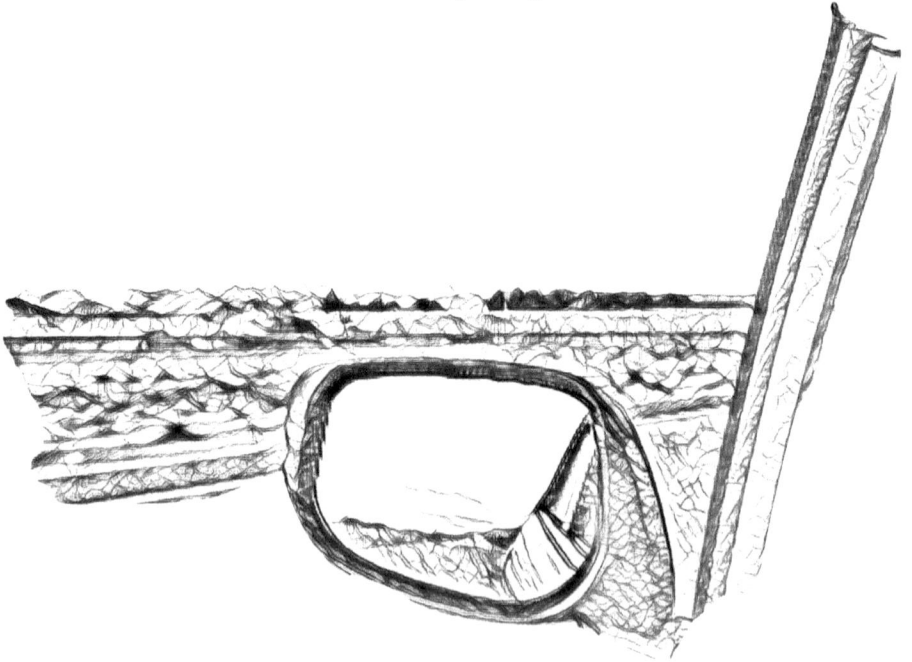

i let myself be held
in the arms of other men
hoping to feel the warmth
i once found in yours
but no pair of hands
has made the point to cradle
the soul beyond these limbs
like you did

-so i sleep alone

JOANNE DZIERZA

i found space near him
to rest my head
but as of late
i have not slept
you can't deny
when it feels like home
and with him i know
i'm a visitor

-the one after you

forgive me if i don't fall
for every compliment
or display of affection
i've learned the tricks
and faux antics
of a lust
disguised as love

-undesired attention

go on darling feel it all
deep in every space
in that crevasse there
let it play
feel it pass through
like fleeting company
greet it like a lover
this uncertainty
and in the moment
of your greatest wavering
let yourself come undone
into the hands of chaos
find yourself through the haze
peace in the discovery
that you're not in control
you will be alright
go on darling
feel it all

-feelings

i imagine in all its years
the earth has seen
no greater let down
than the love
we're forced to keep

-unrequited

another day
carrying the weight
balancing the freedom
and fear of being alone

-you'll be okay

i wonder if God
pines for a soulmate
i imagine the universe
is a lonely place
echoing the loudest silence

-eternal solitude

it was so easy
falling in love with you
why is it so hard to fall out

-trying

i feared the loss of you
picturing a desolate air
but you're never really gone
traces of you visit
like wind through my hair

-you are in the breeze

no matter how quiet
the undercurrent
of our love becomes
there is a beat
that keeps us in sync
and on my days
of greatest need
i will listen for it

-hearts in harmony

sometimes i think
the moon was made just for me
partners in the night
keeping each other
company

-never alone

JOANNE DZIERZA

i didn't want to give up on us
i never thought i'd grow tired
but darling we are such a mess
i feel like we've expired

-expiration date

tonight i give up
on pushing immovable rocks
or changing cemented circumstances
instead
i'll grow a garden
in recognition
of the muscles acquired
from trying

-stronger now

sometimes i wake up
and i'm not devastated
to find myself alone
i call those lucky days
progress

-one day at a time

i guess i'll learn to grow alone
i'll bear the lonely bloom
just don't be shocked if you return
and my garden has no room

-my garden

thank you for the space
you left behind
it is a reminder
of how much room
i have left to grow into

-still growing

of all the heartbreakers
and men who left me behind
you were the best of them
it's an honour to have you written
on these fractured pieces of mine
after all, it was you who taught me
i have everything necessary
to put myself back together in time

-gratitude

how do you know
when you've fallen out of love?
there is no formula, no rule of thumb
it succeeds slowly under the surface
until one day
you catch yourself astonished
at all the details you've forgotten

-coffee orders

IT IS WHAT IT IS

it begins
and it ends
i'm happy
i got to spend
a little bit of
the middle with you

-a life worth living

it's okay
to take chances
and walk the line of ruin
to fall to pieces
and brave the darkness
your victories will succeed
far beyond your knowledge

-the ripples of courage

this is how i heal
letters marching out in single f i l e
and though i'll never write
anything as deep as our love
every word that i spit out
is an attempt to move on

-freedom in words

i bruised my heels
on the road to truth
scarred my knees
for fallacies
spent lonely nights
searching for virtue
embraced passionate nights
in spite of it
i had to painfully unfold
and reshape the roots of me
but i finally arrived
with tear soaked cheeks
at the feet of authenticity

-the journey

i don't wait around
to be loved anymore
i learned how
to do it myself instead
and i'll be damned
if anyone thinks
they could do
a better job
than i can

-love yourself

the end
———

www.ingramcontent.com/pod-product-compliance
Lightning Source LLC
Chambersburg PA
CBHW070616050426
42450CB00011B/3066